Are You My Lover?
Journal

YOUR SPACE FOR REFLECTION,
SOUL NOTES, AND SELF-LOVE.

BY DR. KEZIA SHINE

WELCOME TO YOUR JOURNAL

This journal is your sanctuary, a safe and playful space to hold the reflections, realizations, and truths that rise within you as you walk through ARE YOU MY LOVER? The workbook will guide you with prompts and exercises, while this journal is here for your freedom. There are no rules, no expectations, no "right" way to use it.

Here you can:

- Capture insights from the workbook that you want to expand on.

- Write letters to yourself or to past partners that you never send.

- Record dreams, synchronicities, or memories that surface as you move through the archetypes.

- Doodle, sketch, or express feelings in ways words cannot hold.

- Pour your gratitude, your grief, your joy, and your breakthroughs onto the page.

Think of this journal as a mirror. It will not judge what you place here. It will only reflect your courage to look within and honor your process. Each word, each scribble, each tear that falls on these pages is part of your healing journey.

Take your time. Return often. Let these pages become a container for the most important love story you will ever live - the one with yourself.

REFLECTIONS

"Every person you meet is a mirror."

SOUL NOTES

"*Your greatest love story is within yourself.*"

Mirror Musings

"Love should never make you feel small."

LETTERS TO MYSELF

*"You are not searching for love,
you are remembering that you are love."*

REFLECTIONS

"Love begins the moment I meet myself."

SOUL NOTES

"My truth is the light that guides me."

MIRROR MUSINGS

"I am the mirror and the medicine."

LETTERS TO MYSELF

"Wholeness is who I've been all along."

REFLECTIONS

"Healing begins when you stop running from yourself.

SOUL NOTES

"You are the love you've been searching for."

Mirror Musings

"Every ending is a doorway back to yourself?

LETTERS TO MYSELF

"When you see yourself clearly, the world changes."

REFLECTIONS

When I meet my reflection with compassion,
I meet Spirit within me.

SOUL NOTES

"Each person I attract carries a message from my own soul."

MIRROR MUSINGS

"The mirror doesn't lie—
it reveals where love is still learning to flow."

LETTERS TO MYSELF

*"What I resist in others is the very lesson
I've come here to embrace."*

REFLECTIONS

"Every trigger is an invitation to see where love still fears to go."

SOUL NOTES

"The shadow speaks softly;
it only screams when I refuse to listen."

MIRROR MUSINGS

"In every heartbreak, a piece of myself returns home."

LETTERS TO MYSELF

"Healing is remembering that even my darkness deserves light."

REFLECTIONS

"Your shadows are not flaws, they are invitations."

SOUL NOTES

"Love is not something you chase, it's something you embody."

MIRROR MUSINGS

"You are worthy of love that stays, even when the music ends."

LETTERS TO MYSELF

"The mirror never lies, it shows you the love waiting inside."

REFLECTIONS

"Every heartbreak is a stepping stone back to wholeness."

SOUL NOTES

"You are not too much, you are exactly enough."

MIRROR MUSINGS

*"The way you speak to yourself
becomes the way you love yourself."*

LETTERS TO MYSELF

"True love allows you to grow, not shrink."

REFLECTIONS

"My reflection is my teacher, not my judge."

SOUL NOTES

"The parts of me I once hid have become the wisest voices within."

MIRROR MUSINGS

"When I stop chasing love, I begin magnetizing it."

LETTERS TO MYSELF

*"The person who hurt me the most
became the portal to my awakening."*

REFLECTIONS

*"Every mirror moment is an initiation
into greater self-acceptance."*

SOUL NOTES

"The light in me expands each time I love a part I once rejected."

MIRROR MUSINGS

*"Healing is not linear, it's a dance
between remembering and forgetting."*

LETTERS TO MYSELF

"When I forgive my reflection, my world forgives me too."

REFLECTIONS

"Your soul has always known the way home."

SOUL NOTES

"Every lesson is love in disguise."

MIRROR MUSINGS

"You do not have to earn love, you already are love."

LETTERS TO MYSELF

"Even your broken pieces shine with beauty."

REFLECTIONS

"The shadow holds the keys to my liberation."

SOUL NOTES

*"Wholeness is born
when I stop dividing myself into right and wrong."*

MIRROR MUSINGS

"There's power in seeing my reflection without needing to fix it."

LETTERS TO MYSELF

"Each breath softens the walls I built to protect my heart."

REFLECTIONS

"Peace is a form of love, too."

SOUL NOTES

"You are the sanctuary you've been seeking."

MIRROR MUSINGS

"Love yourself so deeply that others are reminded to do the same."

LETTERS TO MYSELF

"Coming home to yourself is the greatest adventure of all."

REFLECTIONS

"My triggers aren't punishments, they're invitations to grow."

SOUL NOTES

"I no longer search for the one, I remember that I am the one."

MIRROR MUSINGS

"Every ending is love transforming into a higher truth."

LETTERS TO MYSELF

"When I witness myself without judgment,
healing happens naturally."

REFLECTIONS

"The love you give yourself sets the tone for all other love."

SOUL NOTES

"Every time you choose yourself, you heal an old wound."

MIRROR MUSINGS

"Silence often carries the answers your soul has been whispering."

LETTERS TO MYSELF

"Your worth is not up for debate - it simply is."

REFLECTIONS

"Even my shadow is sacred, it taught me how to see the light."

SOUL NOTES

"The soul doesn't shame, it simply shines where the heart is closed."

MIRROR MUSINGS

"My reflection is the altar, my awareness is the prayer."

LETTERS TO MYSELF

"The love I offer myself rewrites every old story."

REFLECTIONS

"Love is not found in perfection, but in presence."

SOUL NOTES

"Every tear waters the soil of our becoming."

MIRROR MUSINGS

"You are allowed to take up spack, just as you are."

LETTERS TO MYSELF

"Even in your darkest moments, your light never goes out."

REFLECTIONS

"Growth happens in the quiet moments after the storm."

SOUL NOTES

"Each version of me was trying to love in the only way it knew how."

MIRROR MUSINGS

"When I see myself as whole, I stop attracting lessons in pieces."

LETTERS TO MYSELF

"The mirror asks only for honesty, not perfection."

REFLECTIONS

*"Wholeness is not about fixing yourself,
it's about embracing yourself."*

SOUL NOTES

"Your heart is both the compass and the destination."

MIRROR MUSINGS

"Boundaries are love notes to your future self."

LETTERS TO MYSELF

"Every mirror you meet reflects an invitation to love deeper."

REFLECTIONS

"In every shadow, there's a spark of light waiting to be noticed."

SOUL NOTES

"I no longer chase validation, I offer myself truth."

MIRROR MUSINGS

"Healing begins when I let myself feel what I once avoided."

LETTERS TO MYSELF

"My reflection changes as my self-love deepens."

WITH LOVE,
DR. SHINE

www.drshinekc.com

www.ingramcontent.com/pod-product-compliance
Lightning Source LLC
Chambersburg PA
CBHW052129030426
42337CB00028B/5079